Praise for *My Love St*

M000204990

"Netanel Miles-Yépez' translations soar with the erotic ecstasy of holy desire, reminding us that knowing God isn't only a matter of emptying out, but also a matter of merging with. His Song sings, and invites you to sing along."

— Rabbi Rami Shapiro, author of *Embracing the Divine Feminine: Song of Songs Annotated and Explained*

"Trust a contemplative to translate a deeply mystical text; better yet, a contemplative with literary ability. Netanel Miles-Yépez combines these and other talents to illuminate the eternally fascinating Song of Songs."

— Sheikh Kabir Helminski, author of *The Knowing Heart: A Sufi Path of Transformation,* and translator of Rumi

"*My Love Stands Behind a Wall* is at once dusk-belonging and dawn-tender. The poems awaken us to an earthy and divine passion that is as real as it is contemporary. There is not a hair of awkwardness to the translations. They are fluid, seamless, and honey-filled. . . . Each flood-splendid verse is a budding thou, a homebound train, a soft world's kiss."

— Josh Goldberg, author of *A Beggar at the Door: Longer and Shorter Psalms*

"These translations burn with mystical intensity and shine with luminous awareness. Highly recommended."

— Mirabai Starr, translator of *Dark Night of the Soul*

my love stands behind a wall

a translation of the song of songs and other poems

second expanded edition

by
netanel miles-yépez

Albion Andalus

Boulder, Colorado

2018

"The old shall be renewed,
and the new shall be made holy."
— Rabbi Avraham Yitzhak Kook

Albion-Andalus, Inc.
P. O. Box 19852
Boulder, CO 80308
www.albionandalus.com

Design and composition by Albion-Andalus, Inc.

Cover design by Sari Wisenthal-Shore

Cover image of the painting, "My Sister, My Bride" by
    Netanel Miles-Yépez. Henna design by Moriah Ferrús

Ink paintings in the text by Netanel Miles-Yépez

Translator's photo by Hilary Benas, 2015

Manufactured in the United States of America

ISBN-13: 978-0692478974 (Albion-Andalus Books)
ISBN-10: 0692478973

for my love
behind a wall

many waters
cannot quench love
nor can floods drown it
for love is as strong as death
passion as cruel as the grave
its flashes are flashes of fire
the very flame of god

contents

acknowledgments

To Jennifer Phares, who originally encouraged me to complete this project, and who gave me the support and freedom to do it, I am forever grateful.

To Puran Bair, Tessa Bielecki, Adam Bucko, Lisa Chatham, David Denny, Michael Gregory, Zvi Ish-Shalom, Nataraja Kallio, Stanley Keleman, Abby Larson, Brett Larson, Sarah Leila Manolson, Matisyahu, Rory McEntee, Rose Yépez Miles, Timothy Miles-Yépez, Atum O'Kane, Mia Seymour, Raj Seymour, Sigmond Kal Shore, Shirah Szabo, Aurora Yépez Wallace, and Sari Wisenthal-Shore, who gave me support in a difficult time.

I also wish to thank the students in my "Religion and Mystical Experience" course at Naropa University in the Spring of 2016 in which I used the first edition of this text to teach a class on mystical poetry which formed the basis of the new Afterword on mystical interpretations of imagery from the Song of Songs, especially Daniel Battigalli-Ansell and Yasha Wagner; Eve Ilsen, for her unforgettable kindness to me, her friendship, and for introducing me to the meanings inherent in the trope of *Shir HaShirim;* Lasette Brown, my dear friend and study buddy, for her tremendous support, and help with an adjective or two; Samantha Krezinski, for taking care of all the other work that allowed me to focus on this project, and who, along with others, had fun ideas for a "forbidden fruit" edition.

And finally, to Nakachi Clark-Kasimu and Deepa Gulrukh Patel, poets, friends, and fellow explorers in the terrain of love, who read the manuscript and provided me with helpful feedback; to Jennifer Alia Wittman, my friend-beloved through the darkest time of my life, my joy, who also read the manuscript and later inspired me to expand and refine the section of mystical poetry, translating more of the poetry of Juan de la Cruz, and to write the Afterword; and to Stella K. Bonnie, who helped me to edit the original introduction, who made the brilliant suggestion for the right and left justification of the male and female speaking parts, and who also made important suggestions on the translation of the Song of Songs.

— N.M.Y.

introduction

The Song of Songs *(Shir HaShirim)*, attributed to the biblical king, Solomon, is among the most beloved and often translated books of the Hebrew Bible. It is beloved both for the beauty of its language and for the religious ideas it has inspired. However, many new readers are often surprised to learn that it has no explicit religious content whatsoever, that it is actually an unabashed celebration of erotic love, i.e., love expressed in terms of desire. So the question naturally arises: how did such an obviously erotic work ever come to enter the canons of Jewish and Christian sacred literature?

In the Jewish tradition, the 2nd-century debate over the matter is recorded in the Mishnah, where some of the sages actually declare the Song of Songs "unclean," unfit to stand beside the sacred histories of their people and the divine commandments given them. But Rabbi Akiva, one of the greatest sages of the era, defends the work, saying: "All the writings of the tradition are holy, but the Song of Songs is the Holiest of the Holies." (Mishnah Yadayim 3:5). Thus it came to be included in the Jewish canon as an allegory for the relationship between God 'the bridegroom' and Israel 'the bride' (while Christians accepted it as an allegorical description of the relationship between Christ and the Church).

In this way, the Song of Songs eventually came to be accepted among the most conservative elements within the Jewish and Christian traditions. And yet, an uneasy tension has always existed between its erotic content and the allegorical interpretation given it, causing many self-appointed guardians of tradition to want to shield 'the uninitiated' from its more suggestive language. In various translations of the Song of Songs through the centuries, this desire has sometimes led well-intentioned translators—whether consciously or unconsciously—to sanitize its content, or to add an interpretive layer to it in order to highlight the allegorical meaning.

As a teacher of religion, I have no objection to the allegorical interpretation of the Song of Songs, especially when one considers how profoundly it has influenced both the language and mystical thought of Christianity and Judaism. Indeed, the mystical poetry inspired by it, including that of Juan de la Cruz (St. John of the Cross), Yehudah Halevi, and Elazar Azikri, is among the most beautiful in these traditions, and is translated here as an example of that influence. But if the Song of Songs is to live on as a source of inspiration for new generations of non-Hebrew readers, I believe its translations should remain as close to the raw eroticism of the original Hebrew as possible, and free of religiously-based assumptions; for it is only in an engagement with its earthy immediacy that direct and spontaneous mystical associations are made in the first place.*

---

* Although something is always lost in translating from one language to another, the imposition of a predetermined interpretation actually distances the reader from the substance and more ambiguous tension of meanings found in the original that can give birth to genuine insights.

Moreover, in allowing it to be what it really is—*love poetry*—we may actually find that we have done another service to religion. For, in overlooking, omitting, or translating-out the racier content of the Song of Songs, the guardians of tradition have only served to perpetuate the erroneous view that the Bible is really a prudish and irrelevant book to one's everyday life. Instead, translations of the Song of Songs should remind people that the Hebrew Bible is not actually a book of 'religion'—not precisely, at least—but a compendium of ancient Hebrew culture: history, myth, literature, poetry, philosophy, prophecy, law, and songs. As such, it is an integral part of the record of human history, and therefore as useful to know and explore as any of the great works of antiquity.

In terms of its style and presentation, the Song of Songs might be described as 'biblical drama,' as it gives one the impression of a dramatic performance from the classical world: the two lovers exchange praise, describe past encounters and current feelings, speak in asides to the audience, and occasionally respond to exhortations and questions from friends and acquaintances.

Beyond this simple description, it is difficult to say much about the storyline of the poem as a whole, or to speak definitively of almost any part of it. This is due in part to the many shifts of speaker in the poem. Often, the reader has no idea who is speaking, or to whom. As already mentioned, not only do the two lovers take turns praising one another, but suddenly turn aside to talk to others who come forward to question each like a Greek chorus.

Furthermore, it is not always clear that it is the same two lovers in dialogue from one part of the poem to the next. Though it is sometimes suggested that the male lover is the king, often identified as Solomon himself, at others times his identity is more ambiguous. And though the female lover is occasionally portrayed as the bride of the king, elsewhere she seems to be a concubine in the king's 'household,' or simply an illicit love. Sometimes the various female voices seem to be those of the women of Solomon's household, trading tales of love and amorous encounters with the king or other lovers. In the end, all we know for certain is that these are the voices of lovers telling the ancient story of love.

As an inexperienced (admittedly amateur) translator of Biblical Hebrew, I quickly learned that, in addition to the aforementioned ambiguities, there are some Hebrew words and phrases whose meanings are unclear even to the most erudite scholar of the language. Thus, a measure of personal interpretation was unavoidable, and indeed, necessary for presenting the poem in a cohesive and coherent way for the modern reader. Nevertheless, I tried to keep such interpretations to a minimum, here and there providing some context for what I thought might be happening at a given point in the poem.

This was accomplished mostly through interpolations, adding italic text in parentheses that suggest possible speakers and to whom they might be speaking. Frequent changes of speaker and direction of address are common in ancient verse, but can be disconcerting for modern readers. Thus, I also chose to provide the reader with visual cues, such as left justification for female voices, right justification for male voices, and centered text for the chorus.

Finally, in translating 'the feel' of the poem, I was guided by one lover's voice in particular. It was she who inspired me to undertake the translation in the first place, and who never left my mind as I worked. Her voice is clear and compelling in the last chapter of the Song. There, a lover who cannot meet with Solomon openly asks him to set her "as a seal" upon his heart, even as they are divided by circumstances. It is she who tells us with depth and gravity that "love is as strong as death" and "passion as cruel as the grave," that her love can neither be bought nor sold. She tells us that Solomon has a vineyard so valuable that he has to post guards to protect its harvest, for it is worth a thousand pieces of silver. Then she says of herself:

i have a vineyard
which is mine alone
to solomon i give
the thousandth part

Somehow, this stands out to me from everything else in the Song, standing apart from the more youthful declarations of love that say, "I am my beloved's and my beloved is mine." Beautiful as that is in its ideal, there is another more mature beauty here in how this particular woman declares herself the owner of her own "vineyard," and how it is she who chooses to whom to grant a share.

To Solomon she gives "the thousandth part," but it is she who makes the choice with an awareness of her own value, and out of love for a man she considers worthy of it. There is no other voice quite like hers in the poem, and it is fitting that this celebration of erotic love should end with her more sober reflections on both the pain of love, and its pleasures, its joy, and its sadness.

— Netanel Miles-Yépez
Boulder, Colorado
August 2nd, 2015

the song of songs
of solomon

for sabiha

1

your love is
better than wine

(to him)

give me the kisses
of your mouth
for your love is *
better than wine

sweet the fragrance
of your ointments
your very name
is anointing to me
thus the young women
love you

take me with you
let's run away
bring me o king
into your room

---

* *Dodeykha,* "your love," refers to *dodim,* the physical careses of love-making.

(the women sing)

we rejoice
and delight in you
your love
is better than wine

(she says to him)

rightly
do they love you

(she says to the women)

i am dark but pleasing
daughters of jerusalem
like the tents of kedar
or the curtains of solomon

do not stare
because i'm dark
the sun's gaze was long on me
for my siblings resented me
making me the keeper
of the vineyards
but my own vineyard
i have not kept

(to him)

tell me
love of my soul
where you feed
where you graze your sheep
where they rest at noon
for why should i
be like a stray
among the flocks
of your companions

(to her)

if you don't know
loveliest of women
then follow the flock
and feed your kids
by the shepherds' tents

my darling
you are like a mare
among pharaoh's chariots

your cheeks
so pleasing
with your hair
in plaits upon them
your neck
laced with jewels

we will add
garlands of gold
to your bangles
of silver

(she says)

while the king
lay on his divan
the fragrance
of my amber oils
was released

my beloved is lodged
like a bundle of myrrh
between my breasts

my beloved
is as a spray
of henna blossoms
from the vineyards
of en-gedi

(to her)

how lovely
my darling
how lovely you are
with eyes like doves

(she responds)

how handsome you are
and pleasing my beloved
our bed a bower of green

our bed chamber beams
of fragrant cedar
our rafters of cypress

2

*rise my love
my beauty
and come away*

(to him)

i am a rose of sharon
a lily of the valleys

(he responds)

as a lily among thorns
is my love among women

(she says)

like an apple tree
in the midst of the forest
is my beloved among men
i sit in his shade with delight
and taste of his fruit sweet

he brought me
into the banquet hall
and his banner over me
was love

sustain me with sweets
refresh me with apples
for i am sick with love

his left arm
under my head
his right arm
embraced me

daughters of jerusalem
by the gazelles
or deer of the field
i charge you
do not awaken
or arouse love
until it's right

listen
my beloved
comes leaping
on the mountains
bounding on the hills

my beloved
is like a gazelle
or a young stag
look he stands
behind our wall
gazing through
the window
peering through
the lattice
my beloved spoke
and said to me

(her beloved said)

rise my love
my beauty
and come away

for winter is past
and the rain is over

flowers dance on the earth
it's time for singing
the song of the turtledove
is filling the land

figs are forming on the tree
and the vines in blossom
giving forth their fragrance

arise my darling
my lovely one
and come away

my dove
in the clefts
of the rocks
hidden by the cliffs
let me see your face
let me hear your voice
for it is sweet
and your face
so lovely

catch us the foxes
the little foxes
that ruin the vines
for our vineyard
is in bloom

(she says)

my beloved is mine
and i am his
who feeds
among the lilies

until day breaks
and shadows flee
turn to me my beloved
and be like a gazelle
or a young stag
on hills of spices

3

on my bed at night
i sought him

on my bed at night
i sought him
whom my soul loves
i sought him
but found him not

i will arise now
and roam the city
through its streets
and squares
i will seek him
whom my soul loves

i sought him
but found him not

the watchmen
who patrol the city
found me thus

my love stands behind a wall

(to the watchmen)

have you seen the one
whom my soul loves

(to us)

scarcely had i passed them
when i found him
whom my soul loves

i held him
and would not let him go
until i had brought him
into my mother's house
into the bedchamber of she
who had conceived me

daughters of jerusalem
by the gazelles
or deer of the field
i do charge you
do not awaken
or arouse love
until it's right

(into the distance)

who is this
that comes up
from the desert
like a pillar of smoke
a cloud of incense
fragrant like all
the merchant's powders

there is solomon's divan
enclosed by sixty warriors
the strength of israel

all of them with sword
and trained to war
swords to guard against
the terrors of the night

the palanquin of king solomon
was made of wood from lebanon

its poles of silver
its roof of gold
its cushions purple
inlaid with love
by the daughters
of jerusalem

daughters of zion
gaze on the king
solomon crowned
with that which
his mother gave him
on his wedding day
his day of heartful joy

4
behold
you are lovely

(to her)

you are lovely
my darling
you are lovely
your eyes behind
your veil like doves
your hair like
a flock of goats
trailing down
mount gilead

your teeth like
a flock of ewes
all shaped alike
come up from
the washing pool
paired and none missing

your lips like
a ribbon of scarlet
your mouth lovely
behind your veil
your cheeks
pomegranates

your neck like
the tower of david
a turret necklaced
with thousands
of tiny shields
the woven armor
of mighty warriors

your breasts
like two fawns
twin gazelles made
to feed among the lilies

until day breaks
and shadows flee
i will take me to
the mountain of myrrh
the hill of incense

every part of you
is lovely my darling
there is nothing in you
that is not perfection

come with me
from lebanon
from lebanon
come with me
my bride
to look from
the heights of amana
the peaks of
senir and hermon
from the lions' dens
and leopard hills

you have ravished so
my heart my sister my bride
you have ravished so
my heart with just one of your eyes
with a single braid of your necklace

how lovely
your affection
my sister my bride
how much sweeter
your love than wine
your ointments
more fragrant
than any spice

honey drops sweet
from your lips my bride
milk and honey
are under your tongue
the scent of your robes
the fragrance of lebanon

an enclosed garden
is my sister my bride
a fountain covered
a spring sealed up

the shoots of your limbs
an orchard of pomegranates
full with precious fruits
decorated with henna
and amber oils

spikenard tendrils
and saffron threads
fragrant wetland reeds
and cinnamon bark
an aromatic wood
of myrrh and aloes
every choice perfume

you are a garden spring
a well of living waters
a stream out of lebanon

(she says)

north wind awake
south wind come
blow upon my garden
and spread its perfume
that my beloved may
come to his garden
and enjoy its fruit

5

*i sleep
but my heart
is awake*

(he says)

i have come
to my garden
my sister my bride
i have gathered
myrrh and spice
i have eaten
honeycomb and honey
i have drunk
wine and milk

(friends say)

eat and drink friends
drink your fill of love

(she tells us)

i sleep
but my heart
is awake

listen
my beloved knocks

(he says)

open to me
my sister
my love undefiled
for my head
is covered with dew
my locks with
the drops of the night

(she responds)

i've taken off my robe
must i put it on again
i have washed my feet
shall i soil them now

(she tells us)

my beloved put his hand
through the keyhole
and my insides
quivered for him

i rose to open
to my beloved
my hands
dripped with myrrh
my fingers
with flowing myrrh
upon the lock

i opened
to my beloved
but my beloved
had turned away
and was gone
my heart
had gone out to him

when he spoke
i could not find him
i called to him
but he answered not

the watchmen
who patrol the city
found me thus
and abused me
the keepers of the wall
tore my mantle from me

i charge you
daughters of jerusalem
if you find my beloved
tell him that i'm
sick with love

(they answer)

how is your beloved
better than others
loveliest of women
how is your beloved
better than others
that you charge us so

(she says)

my beloved
is white and ruddy
set above ten thousand
his face is as fine gold

his locks curled
black as a raven

his eyes like doves
beside the waters
washed with milk
and well set

his cheeks are
as a bed of spices
as banks of sweet herbs
his lips are as lilies
dripping with
flowing myrrh

his arms are
as sturdy rods of gold
set with beryl
his body like
polished ivory
overlaid with sapphires

his legs are
as pillars of marble
set upon sockets
of fine gold
his aspect like lebanon
excellent as its cedars

his mouth is so sweet
he is altogether lovely

this is my beloved
this is my friend
daughters of jerusalem

6

where has your
beloved gone

(they ask)

where has your beloved gone
loveliest of women
where has your beloved turned
that we may seek him with you

(she says)

my beloved
has gone down
into his garden
to the bed of spices
to feed in the garden
and gather lilies

i am my beloved's
and my beloved is mine
who feeds among the lilies

(he says)

you are lovely
my darling as tirzah
becoming as jerusalem
daunting as an army
arrayed for battle

turn your gaze
from me please
'fore it overwhelms me

your hair is like
a flock of goats
trailing down
gilead's heights

your teeth like
a flock of ewes
all shaped alike
climbing from
the washing pool
paired together
and none missing

behind your veil
your cheeks
pomegranates

there are sixty queens
and eighty concubines
and damsels uncounted

only one is my perfect dove
unique from her mother
delight of she who bore her
praised by the damsels who see
approved by queens and concubines

who is she
rising like the dawn
lovely as the moon
radiant as the sun
daunting as an army
arrayed for battle

i descended
into the nut grove
to see the budding valley
the vines in blossom
the pomegranates in flower

before i knew it
my soul was harnessed
to the whim of a noble chariot

7

come back
come back

(they cry)

come back
come back shulamite
come back come back
that we may look on you again

(they ask him)

what do you see
in this shulamite woman
that she appears as a dance
between two armies

(to her)

how lovely
your sandaled feet
gentleman's daughter
your thighs round
like teardropped pearls
the work of a skilled artisan

your navel a round goblet
never lacking in wine
your belly a heap of wheat
set about with lilies

your breasts like
two fawns twin gazelles

your neck a tower of ivory
your eyes pools in heshbon
by the gate of bat-rabbim
your nose the tower of lebanon
that looks toward damascus

your head a crown
like mount carmel
your hair like purple royal
the king held captive
in your tresses

how lovely how pleasing
my love full of delights

your body like a palm tree
your breasts clusters of grapes

i said i will climb this palm
and take hold of its branches
your breasts like clusters of the vine
your face fragrant of apples

your mouth wet
with the best of wine
running smoothly
over your lips my beloved
opening gently
like those of sleepers

(she says)

i am my beloved's
and his desire is for me

(to him)

come my beloved
let's go into the field
and spend the night
among the henna

let's go early
to the vineyards
to see whether the vines
do blossom
the pomegranates
flower

37

i will give you
my love there

the mandrake root
gives its fragrance
and at our doors
all manner
of precious fruit
both freshly picked
and long stored
have i laid up
for you alone
my beloved

8

set me as a seal
on your heart

(to him)

if only
you were as a brother
who had nursed
at my mother's breast
then i could meet you
in the open and kiss you
and none would despise me

i would lead you
i would bring you
into my mother's house
and you would instruct me
i'd let you drink
of the spiced wine
the juice of my
pomegranate

(to herself)

his left arm under my head
his right hand caressed me

(to the young women)

i charge you
daughters of jerusalem
do not awaken or arouse love
until its time is right

(people ask)

who is she
that comes up from the desert
leaning on her beloved

(she says to him)

under
the apple tree
i aroused you
it was there
your mother
conceived
she who bore you
conceived

set me as a seal
on your heart
like the seal
upon the ring
of your hand

for love is as strong as death
passion as cruel as the grave

its flashes
are flashes of fire
the very flame of god

many waters
cannot quench love
nor can floods drown it
if you offered
all your wealth for love
you would be
laughed to scorn

(the women say)

we have a little sister
whose breasts are small
what will we do for her
on the day she is claimed

if she be as a wall
we will build turrets
of silver upon her
if she be as a door
we will panel her
with carven cedar

41

my love stands behind a wall

(she says)

i am a fortress wall
my breasts towers upon it
so i became in his eyes
one who finds favor

solomon had once
a vineyard in baal-hamon
a vineyard to which
he had to post guards
for its harvest was worth
a thousand pieces of silver

i have a vineyard
which is mine alone
to solomon i give
the thousandth part
and its guardians
a two-hundredth

(to all)

you who linger
in the gardens
lovers are listening
let me hear your voice

(to him)

hurry my beloved
swift as a gazelle
or a young stag
to the hills of spices

poems
of mystical love
inspired by the
song of songs

for alia

the spiritual canticle
by
juan de la cruz

(the bride)

where have you hidden love
leaving me to wail
having wounded me
you fled like a stag
and i followed after
crying aloud
but you were gone

shepherds as you travel
with your flocks on the hills
if by chance you should see
the one whom i love most
tell him i suffer sicken and die

i'll head for the mountains
seeking out my love
at the edge of streams
i'll not stop to gather flowers
nor yield to fear of animals
i'll pass the strong
and go beyond the bounds

tell me
woods and bushes
planted by my love
green meadows
bright with flowers
has he passed here

spilling blessings
by the thousands
he passed these groves
moving quickly
with his countenance alone
clothed them in beauty
as he looked on them

who now
has the power to heal me
surrender yourself wholly now
don't send any more messengers
they can't tell me
what i need to hear

the liberated will tell me
a thousand blessed things of you
each wounding me unto death
from an unknown sickness
caught from their stammerings

life how do you endure
living not where you live
brought down and near death
from the piercing arrows
of your thoughts of the beloved

why don't you heal
this heart you wounded
why don't you take away
what you've already stolen

extinguish this misery
which only you can quell
allow my eyes to see you
you their very light
you alone for whom
i would open them

crystalline springtime
if only your dewy shimmer
would form a living face
opening the eyes i desire to see
the eyes engraved on my heart

take them from me love
for i am taking flight

(the bridegroom)

return my dove
the wounded stag
is in sight of the hill
soothed by the breeze
of your flight

(the bride)

my love is the mountain
the lonely wooded vale
an exotic island
a roaring river
an amorous breeze
calling

the night tranquil
before the dawn awakening
silent music solitude sounding
a restoring meal deepening love

our bed is flowering
encircled by lions' dens
established in peace
draped in purple
crowned with a thousand
shields of gold

following in your footsteps
the young women run
sap coursing in them divine
like spiced wine and electricity

in the wine-cellar within
i drank of my beloved
but going out into the valley
i no longer knew anything
and lost the herd i'd followed

there he gave me his breast
and delicious understanding
i gave myself to him
holding nothing back
and promised to be his bride

now i employ my soul
all my energy in his service
i tend the herd no longer
nor have i any other work
now that all my acts are love

if i am no longer found
out and about with others
you will say that i am lost
indeed i lost myself
stricken by love
and was found

with flowers and emeralds
chosen in the fresh morning air
we'll weave garlands
in your love flowering
bound with a single hair of mine

you looked on a single strand
dangling loose at my neck
gazing at it captivated
wounded by just one of my eyes

you looked at me
and your eyes
inscribed your grace on me
you loved me passionately
thus my eyes deserved to adore
what they beheld in you

if i was dark before
don't despise me
look on me now
you've left grace
and beauty in me
with your gaze

let us catch the foxes
now that our vineyard is in flower
let us make a cone of roses
to rival that of the pine
and let no one appear on the hill

be still deathly north wind
come south wind awakening love
breathe into the garden
and let its fragrance spread
as my love feeds among the flowers

(the bridegroom)

the bride has come
into the pleasing orchard
of her desire
to rest in delight
laying her neck
on the gentle arms
of her love

under the apple tree
i took you for my own
i offered you my hand
where your mother
was sadly used
i restored you

winged birds
lions stags leaping deer
mountains valleys shores
waters winds heat
fears of night a'watch

by the pleasing lyre
and the siren's song
i conjure you cease your anger
and touch not the wall
to disturb the bride
that she sleep in peace

(the bride)

girls of judea
among flowers and roses
the amber perfume rises
stay you on the borders
don't approach our threshold

hide yourself my love
turn your face to the mountains
and speak not a word
look at the companions
traveling with her
through distant islands

(the bridegroom)

a small white dove
is returned to the ark
with an olive branch
the turtledove has found
its longed-for companion
by the verdant riverbank

in solitude she lived
and in solitude now
has made her a nest
in solitude he guides her
he alone who in solitude
bears the wound of love

(the bride)

rejoice beloved
let's see ourselves in your beauty
going to the mountain and hill
where the pure waters flow
and then into the deep thicket

we'll go on to the high rocks
to the caverns well-concealed
enter and taste the juice
of the pomegranates

there you'll show me
what my soul has sought
you'll give me you my life
there what you gave me before

the breathing of the airs
nightingale song so sweet
the living beauty of the trees
in the night serene with flame
all-consuming and painless

no one looked at her
and aminadab came not
the siege calmed
and the cavalry descended
at the sight of the waters

on a dark night
by
juan de la cruz

on a dark night
enflamed with love
and urgent longing
  oh delightful chance
i went out unseen
my house completely still

in darkness secure
by a ladder secret
  oh delightful chance
in darkness concealed
my house completely still

on that happy night
in secret unseen
looking at nothing
without guide or light
other than the one
in my heart burning

a guide more sure
than the light at midday
to him who awaited me
   to him i knew so well
to a place secluded
where no one else could see

oh guiding night
night more lovely than the dawn
night that unites lover and beloved
transforming the beloved in her lover

upon my flowering breast
which i kept for him alone
he lay sleeping and i caressing him
amid a breeze from swaying cedars

as the air descended
from the battlement
i parted his hair
his serenely gentle hand
wounding my neck
suspending all my senses

i withdrew and forgot myself
i lay my face against the beloved
everything ceased and i left myself
leaving my cares among the lilies forgotten

love and living flame
by
juan de la cruz

love and living flame
how tenderly you wound
in her deepest core my soul
you are no longer shy
so end this if you will
and tear the veil from
this sweet encounter

soothing remedy
coveted wound
gentle hand
delicate touch
knowing life eternal
and paying all debts
      in killing —
death you bring to life

lamps of fire
in whose splendors
the deep caverns of feeling
once so dark and sightless
display now their strange beauties
with light and heat
for their beloved

how gentle and loving
your remembrance in my breast
where in secret you dwell   *alone*
and with your honeyed sigh
healing and gloriously swollen
how tenderly you make me love

of the creation
by
juan de la cruz

'a bride who loves you
i want to give you my son
one who will deserve
to share a life with us
to eat at the same table
that she might know
the goodness of my child
and rejoice with me
in your grace and wholeness'

'i'm grateful father'
responded the son
'to the bride you give
i'll give sincerely
that she might see
the worth of my father
and how i received
the being i possess
from your being
i'll hold her in my arms
and she'll burn with *your love*
and in eternal delight
praise your goodness'

* * *

'it is done then,'
said the father,
'for your love deserves it'
and with these words
the world was created
a palace for the bride
fashioned with wisdom
with two chambers
dividing above and below

the lower contained
an infinity of differences
the upper beautifully
decorated with jewels
so that the bride might
recognize the groom

there on high
the angelic nature
was given a place
but human nature
being a thing lesser
was set lower

though their natures
were divided this way
they all form the bride

for love of the groom
makes them all one

those above in joy
possess the groom
those in hope below
are infused with faith
through his promise

'one day i will lift you up
take you from lowliness
so that none can mock you'

he would become as them
come to dwell among them
god would become human
and human become god
he would talk with them
eat and drink with them
he would be among them
consummating this world

joined together
they will sing
the eternal song
being above the bride
in him he unites all
who form her body

taking her tenderly
enfolded in his arms
he gives her his love
and joined as one
she is elevated
to the divine root
where god's joy
becomes her joy

for the father
and the son
and the one who
proceeds from them
live in one another
and so it will be
with the bride
taken unto god
to live the life of god

the shepherd's pain
by
juan de la cruz

a young shepherd
living in pain and alone
a stranger to contentment
his thoughts on a shepherd-girl
his chest broken open by love

he weeps not
for the wound of love
that is not an affliction
however deep it goes
his tears are for knowing
that he's been forgotten

the very thought that
the lovely shepherd-girl
has forgotten him
is a pain so great
that he suffers torment
like a stranger in a strange land
his breast forever broken
and sundered by love

the shepherd—
'misery
is distance
from my love
who cares not
to be near me
and my chest
broken by love'

after a while
he climbed up
the branches of a tree
opened his beautiful arms
and hung by the branches *dead*
his breast forever broken
and sundered by love

the bride in longing
by
yehudah halevi

she goes out to meet you
the bride in longing
no longer allowed
to worship in your sanctuary
she pines in loneliness for you

embarrassed in her desire
to ascend the holy mount
covered now with strangers
she stands longing from afar
worshipping your temple
from every station of her exile
her pleading an offering to you
hanging her heart and eyes
heavily on your throne
listen now to her cry
calling in the bitterness
of her exhausted heart
and fainting soul

curtains of solomon
by
yehudah halevi

curtains of solomon
amid the tents of kedar
how changed you are
no form no beauty
have you now

legions that once
dwelt in our midst
left us in desolation
an unprotected ruin
our holy vessels
profaned in exile
how can you ask for beauty
now amid the thorns

cast out by neighbors
but sought by their lord
who calls them still by name
not one among them forgotten
their beauty he will restore
in the end as in the beginning
lighting the candelabra
which has since darkened

fever-tossed sleeper
by
yehudah halevi

fever-tossed sleeper
with a heart awake
arise and walk out now
in the light of my face

for a star will rise over you
and the dungeon's prisoner
will ascend to sinai's summit

heed not those who say
'zion is now condemned'
for my heart is there
and my eyes upon it

i reveal and hide myself
angry only in appearance
for who will have pity
on these my children
except me

beloved
of my soul
by
elazar azikri

beloved of my soul
compassion's gentle source
take my heart and shape it
with your desire

then like a deer in flight
i will run to you
and in your presence
i will lay me down

pour your love
sweet upon me
and let me drink my fill
no other wine no honey
will still this thirst for you

splendid is your light
and the worlds reflecting it
my soul is worn thin
from craving warmth
and tender kisses

please god heal her
show her your face
bathed in radiance
surely she will
find her strength
healing and delight
will be hers forever

does pity stir you my god
won't you be kind to me
your own child
begotten of your love

long and longing hours
i've yearned only
for your glance
when shall i see
my light in your light
and bask contented
in your warm embrace

how my heart desires
union with yours
don't hide your pity
don't conceal
your light from me

remember me
my beloved shelter me
under a canopy of peace
cover us in your
delight and presence
and we will rejoice
with song and dance

rush
be quick my love
this is the time
for our union
let your gentle favor
grace us once again *

---

* Based on an earlier translation by Zalman M. Schachter-Shalomi.

friday evening
by
yitzhak luria

sing and praise
enter the gates
of paradise holy

bid her enter
her life and light
with gifts we await

fair bride
surrounded
on right and left
regally wrapped
jeweled abundance

husband embraced
held firm in holiness
blissfully crushed
in ecstasy

surrendered
are the pains
silenced the cries
replaced by joy

new radiance is
bestowed this day
souls added to souls

the walls of delight
are scaled for union
light penetrating them
with blessing

come close now
and entertain her
serve her sweets
from the banquet

soul be the essence
every spirit renewed
in this holy union

seventy crowns on her
holy so holy in glory
the splendor of the king

effulgence hidden
within the worlds
transcending all
and indwelling

i plead with him
to dwell among us
enjoying us sweetly

in the south my banquet
in the light of arcane love
bread in the north abundant

betrothed and lover
feeding one another
sustained with the
fragrance of myrtle

precious sanctification
of holy-numbered words
surrounded indwelling
six loaves skillfully woven
collected on each side

cut off and forsaken
pain and wounds
ugliness banished

break bread then
from each loaf
two points to make
the secret clear

press the olives pure
the oil to flow silently
interior rivers hidden

with secrets to share
words hidden in the dark
thoughts unseen by eyes

i crown you bride so holy
with secrets celestial
from the mating feast
of the angelic hosts [*]

---

[*] Based on an earlier translation by Zalman M. Schachter-Shalomi.

come my beloved
by
shlomo halevi alkabetz

come my beloved
to meet the bride
to see her face
to receive her sabbath

at once god said
observe-remember
that god and god's name
are one with splendid prayer

to meet the sabbath go
a wellspring of blessing
our source of comfort
first and last eternal

majestic city rise
abandon your tears
leave your seat of trouble
embrace god's mercy

rise shake the dust
from your garments
dress yourself in splendor
the hand of jesse of bethlehem
draws the soul's redemption nigh

awaken awaken i say
shine and sing
the glory of god
is revealed in you

let go of your shame
let go of embarrassment
why be downcast and sigh
the poor will find comfort
god's city will be rebuilt

your enemies will fail
the devourers cast out
god will rejoice in you
as a groom in his bride

you will burst forth
and revere your lord
by the hand of phares child
we will rejoice and sing happily

(make ready her dwelling
turn to face the open door)

bring your peace
crown of your husband
bring happiness and joy
to your faithful servants
come bride sabbath queen

afterword

While imprisoned for nine months in 1577, Juan de Yepes y Álvarez, better known as Juan de la Cruz, composed the greater part of his classic poem, *Cántico Espiritual*—'Spiritual Canticle'—inspired by the Song of Songs. In a tiny cell, with barely any food or light to comfort him, he withdrew into an inner world, populated by the imagery of the Song of Songs—a world of mountains and rivers, flora and fauna, and lovers seeking union—a world he knew by heart. As his title suggests, he was very much aware that the "Canticle of Canticles," as it is called in the Catholic Christian tradition, is actually an erotic love poem interpreted allegorically, and thus he calls his own poem, a *"spiritual canticle."* Like mystics all over the world, he understood that the best metaphor for mystical union—*unio mystica*—was the sexual metaphor, and for the shifts and changes of intimate relationship with the Divine, the metaphor of romantic love. It is this metaphor that animates the allegory of bride and groom found in the mystical poetry inspired by the Song of Songs, and which instructs us in the mystical romance between God and humanity.

"The Spiritual Canticle" itself is conceived as a kind of dialogue between separated lovers, a bride, representing humanity, in relation to Christ, the groom, representing

Divinity. The bride calls to her absent lover who has suddenly disappeared:

where have you hidden love
leaving me to wail
having wounded me
you fled like a stag
and i followed after
crying aloud
but you were gone

Just as so often happens in human affairs, the divine lover appears to pull away. Having experienced God's 'kiss,' the mystical experience of divine union, the bride in the person of Juan de la Cruz, is left with a wound of love, whose only remedy is *re-union*. The wound itself is caused by separation, the 'tearing away' from the knowledge of the wholeness experienced in union with the Divine.

The beloved groom who has suddenly disappeared is the hidden God, the *deus absconditus*, hidden from us precisely when most wanted, and so terribly silent to our longing driven lament. The erotic image of the virile stag from the Song of Songs—come to roam on "hills of spices"—is reversed here, and now the stag is the kind which suddenly takes flight after mating for some unknown reason, either frightened by some danger, or drawn to it, or perhaps even drawn to another amorous encounter. The lover is left not knowing where the beloved has gone, or why. Nevertheless, she is committed to her beloved now and sets her course:

i'll head for the mountains
seeking out my love
at the edge of streams
i'll not stop to gather flowers
nor yield to fear of animals
i'll pass the strong
and go beyond the bounds

What is Juan de la Cruz trying to say to us? *'No distractions, no obstacles will stop me now!'* The bride has tasted God's kiss, and will no longer be satisfied with anything less than that. She'll "go beyond the bounds," transcending the ordinary desires. She'll not "stop to gather flowers," the pretty little things of the material world, or even of the spiritual path, the petty delights of 'spiritual materialism' with which most are contented. That's not where she is going to be caught. Nor will she yield to fears. She's going for the deepest possible experience of Divinity, even if it means the obliteration of her own ego in God.

tell me
woods and bushes
planted by my love
green meadows
bright with flowers
has he passed here

This can be taken in two senses: the lover searching everywhere, almost in a frenzy to find and reestablish the relationship with the beloved; but also, having known union with God, and thus God's presence in all creation, we begin to look for and see God in everything around us.

who now
has the power to heal me
surrender yourself wholly now
don't send any more messengers
they can't tell me
what i need to hear

the liberated will tell me
a thousand blessed things of you
each wounding me unto death
from an unknown sickness
caught from their stammerings

Again, having tasted of the Divine directly, having actually had a mystical experience of some sort, she is saying that 'no substitutes or intermediaries will do anymore between you and me.' She doesn't want to hear from the theologians; she doesn't want to read any more books—"They can't tell me what I need to hear." She doesn't even want to hear from the "liberated," the enlightened, the mystics who have been where she has been, because their words only make her more miserable, "wounding me unto death from an unknown sickness caught from their stammerings." They only increase her terrible longing.

life how do you endure
living not where you live
brought down and near death

from the piercing arrows
of your thoughts of the beloved

why don't you heal
this heart you wounded
why don't you take away
what you've already stolen

In separation from the Beloved, it is as if she is living a half-life. Having experienced the fullness of that relationship, life without it feels empty by comparison. This is *'life living not where it lives,'* the soul torn from the body and carried away, in possession now of the absent beloved. Life is with the beloved, and *this*—what is left— is not life. So she says, "Why don't you take away what you've already stolen." *You've stolen my heart, don't leave the rest behind.*

Finally, we hear the groom speak. He describes himself as a "wounded stag":

return my dove
the wounded stag
is in sight of the hill
soothed by the breeze
of your flight

That's all he says, but it turns the whole understanding of the situation upside down. The bride thinks she is the one who is wounded. From her perspective, she has had an experience of union with the groom, with the divine beloved, who then left her and went away. But he is saying the opposite, that it is he who is wounded by her. He is not the stag that ran away; he is saying, 'I'm here, waiting, in plain sight as you flee from me, and I feel the breeze of it.'

It is the contrast of human and divine perspectives. There is an experience of intimacy with the Divine, and when it ends, we feel the absence of it, and cry out: 'God, where have you gone?' But God, on the other end, is saying, 'What do you mean? I'm right here; I haven't gone anywhere. Can't you see me? It is you who have wounded me! You have turned your awareness from me, and it has torn something from my Wholeness; you are torn from my Wholeness. Your consciousness has shifted back to an ordinary state of mind, away from unitive consciousness to a state of separation.'

my love is the mountain
the lonely wooded vale
an exotic island
a roaring river
an amorous breeze
calling

Now the bride speaks again, identifying the divine beloved with nature, everything that she is seeing in nature is now understood to be divine based on her experience. 'This is my beloved . . . This is my beloved . . . And this too.'

the night tranquil
before the dawn awakening

silent music solitude sounding
a restoring meal deepening love

our bed is flowering
encircled by lions' dens
established in peace
draped in purple
crowned with a thousand
shields of gold

The bride is recalling the place of her union with the groom, a bed on the grass in the woods, encircled by lions' dens. She describes all the beauty and danger around it that keeps it pure and sacrosanct. For in that moment of divine union and intimacy, there is nothing else, no one else; it is completely protected, because they are completely unified, one. There are no other thoughts, no distractions. There is nothing to assail that union. While established, it is pure, inviolable, and eternal.

following in your footsteps
the young women run
sap coursing in them divine
like spiced wine and electricity

in the wine-cellar within
i drank of my beloved
but going out into the valley
i no longer knew anything
and lost the herd i'd followed

Tasting the wine in the wine-cellar within is the foray into mystical experience through spiritual practice. But when the practice has opened her to another dimension of experience, she leaves the duality of the practice behind, coming "into the valley," into the place of union, where she can no longer find herself, because there is no longer any concept of a separate self. "I no longer knew anything and lost the herd I'd followed." She had followed a trail into the divine experience, but once there, no longer knew any *thing* in her state of content-less consciousness.

there he gave me his breast
and delicious understanding
i gave myself to him
holding nothing back
and promised to be his bride

now i employ my soul
all my energy in his service
i tend the herd no longer
nor have i any other work
now that all my acts are love

The things of the external world, she claims, are no longer satisfying to her, "nor have I any other work now that all my acts are love."

if i am no longer found
out and about with others
you will say that i am lost

indeed i lost myself
stricken by love
and was found

As the world she knew before is no longer satisfying, she says, 'Don't expect to find me out with my old friends, in the places I used to frequent. I won't be there. I am lost now in my beloved.'

In "On a Dark Night"—*Noche Oscura*—Juan de la Cruz makes the relationship with the divine Beloved at once more essential, more intense, and also more explicit in its reference to a mystical spiritual practice, connecting it with the "Divine Darkness" of Pseudo-Dionysius the Areopagite, as well as the "Cloud of Unknowing" in the terms of the anonymous Middle English mystical classic.

on a dark night
enflamed with love
and urgent longing
    oh delightful chance
i went out unseen
my house completely still

in darkness secure
by a ladder secret
    oh delightful chance
in darkness concealed
my house completely still

Love is rarely licit or completely happy in mystical poetry from this period. Marriage was often arranged, and largely a social contract, so that romantic love wasn't necessarily a part of marriage. Thus, 'true love,' or romantic love, was often depicted as illicit, going against the social norms, because there was no actual reward—you don't really get to have the beloved, you can't really be with them, and all of society and its sanctions are against you. Thus, it was considered, 'true.'* And just as young lovers in the poetry of the troubadours must often overcome numerous obstacles, finding a way to one another—evading parents, guardians, husbands, wives—to meet under the cover of darkness, so too must the mystic lover meet with her divine beloved in the darkness. She moves through the house "in darkness secure," the "house completely still," escaping "by a ladder secret."

The poet, Juan de la Cruz, tells us himself in his commentary that the poem is allegorical, concealing a deeper meaning of mystical significance. So we must ask—What is meant by the quiet house in the dark, and the secret ladder?

From the mystical perspective, the references easily align with the well-known structures and aspects of contemplative practice. The "house completely still" is the body, no longer fidgeting or seeking to move, but settled into the meditative practice, the "ladder" connecting Earth and Heaven. It is the technique of getting into the "Divine Darkness," or the "Cloud of Unknowing," the place of intimacy or union with the Divine, where

---

* A distinction must be made here between illicit love and illicit sex. This example is clearly about the former, though it may include the latter.

our senses fail, where there is no more awareness of a separate self, only the divine Presence.

on that happy night
in secret unseen
looking at nothing
without guide or light
other than the one
in my heart burning

Paying no attention to anything in the external world, the mystic lover withdraws from the senses and focuses on an inner light, fueled by desire burning in the heart. That is to say, the focus is inward, on something placed in the heart, perhaps as *The Cloud of Unknowing* suggests, fixing all our love on God, even using "the word 'God,' the word, 'love,' " as meditative objects, planted like seeds in the heart, over and over.

a guide more sure
than the light at midday
to him who awaited me
    to him i knew so well
to a place secluded
where no one else could see

oh guiding night
night more lovely than the dawn
night that unites lover and beloved
transforming the beloved in her lover

"Oh guiding night," she says; not "Oh guiding light," as we might expect. "Night more lovely than the dawn." Darkness is better than light! For it is the "night that unites lover and beloved, transforming the beloved in her lover." Making love in the darkness, the lover is transformed in union with the beloved. You might say, the beloved flowers inside of her.

upon my flowering breast
which i kept for him alone
he lay sleeping and i caressing him
amid a breeze from swaying cedars

With these few simple lines, Juan de la Cruz paints a beautiful scene of two lovers on a hillside, perhaps on a blanket, describing himself as a young woman, the head of her beloved lying on her "flowering breast," which she has "kept for him alone," "caressing him" as a breeze cools them on a hot summer evening.

These lines, perhaps more than any others in the poetry translated here, bring home for me the boundary-crossing homo-eroticism of the mystical poetry based on the Song of Songs, where love causes the mystic to transcend— almost with abandon (in verse, at least)—the social norms of the time. Because God is the beloved, and assumed to be masculine in the patriarchal, hetero-normative cultures in which this poetry was written, we are the lover, assumed to be feminine. So it is often only when a woman composes poetry of divine love in Abrahamic traditions (as there are exceptions) that the relationship seems conventional at all, the rest of it transcending gender relationship norms and suggesting, "Love is love."

as the air descended
from the battlement
i parted his hair
his serenely gentle hand
wounding my neck
suspending all my senses

Now, continuing with this gentle scene, the divine beloved lying on her breast, reaches a hand up to touch her neck, to caress it. The contact with her skin, thrills her with ecstasy, causing the suspension of all of her limited senses. This is the experience of intimacy with the Divine in the "Divine Darkness," where the senses no longer function. And thus, the poem ends with the lines:

i withdrew and forgot myself
i lay my face against the beloved
everything ceased and i left myself
leaving my cares among the lilies forgotten

In that extraordinary intimacy, there was no longer any sense of separate self, her former cares taking up no more space in her consciousness than the lilies of the hillside, now forgotten by the embracing lovers.

Many of these same tropes are also echoed in the Jewish mystical poetry inspired by the Song of Songs, though expressed in different ways. In "Beloved of My Soul"—

Yedid Nefesh—by the Jewish poet and kabbalist, Elazar
Azikri, the author speaks to God as the soul's advocate,
identifying with his soul, begging compassion for 'she
who loves Him.'

please god heal her
show her your face
bathed in radiance
surely she will
find her strength
healing and delight
will be hers forever

does pity stir you my god
won't you be kind to me
your own child
begotten of your love

Here, the feminine-masculine relationship between
the soul and the Divine is accomplished naturally, as the
Hebrew word for 'soul,' *nefesh*, is itself feminine. Thus,
this famous mystical poem easily takes up the imagery of
the Song of Songs, identifying the soul with the amorous
deer, and the lover partaking of wine and honey with her
beloved.

beloved of my soul
compassion's gentle source
take my heart and shape it
with your desire

then like a deer in flight
i will run to you
and in your presence
i will lay me down

pour your love
sweet upon me
and let me drink my fill
no other wine no honey
will still this thirst for you

The Spanish-Jewish poet, Yehudah Halevi—unlike
Azikri, who deals with the soul's relationship with God—
mostly treats the bride as the Jewish people in exile
from their homeland, cut-off from their holy sanctuary
in Jerusalem. In "Fever-tossed Sleeper," he speaks as a
masculine God to the feminine lover who dreams of
Him, the people of Israel.

heed not those who say
'zion is now condemned'
for my heart is there
and my eyes upon it

i reveal and hide myself
angry only in appearance
for who will have pity
on these my children
except me

And in his "Curtains of Solomon" and "The Bride in Longing" he bemoans the state of the Jewish people in exile and Jerusalem abandoned, pleading the cause of the faithful lover, and making a case with God for their restoration.

she goes out to meet you
the bride in longing
no longer allowed
to worship in your sanctuary
she pines in loneliness for you

embarrassed in her desire
to ascend the holy mount
covered now with strangers
she stands longing from afar
worshipping your temple
from every place of her exile
her pleading an offering to you
hanging her heart and eyes
heavily on your throne
listen now to her cry
calling in the bitterness
of her exhausted heart
and fainting soul

But perhaps the most potent mystical symbolism in the Hebrew poetry based on the Song of Songs is that which identifies the bride with the *Shekhinah*, the divine 'indwelling,' the feminine presence of God in the world. This is a kabbalistic emphasis, reversing the usual roles.

Here, Israel takes the masculine role, courting the divine bride, longing for her Presence among them, identifying Her with the Sabbath—*Shabbat*—where holiness exists in time.

We see this emphasis in Yitzhak Luria's "Friday Evening" and Shlomo Halevi Alkabetz' "Come My Beloved"—*Lekhah Dodi*—traditionally sung at sundown on Friday as the Sabbath descends. The latter calls Jews to ready themselves as a bridegroom prepares for his wedding night, preparing to meet the holy "Sabbath Queen."

come my beloved
to meet the bride
to see her face
to receive her sabbath

. . .

bring your peace
crown of your husband
bring happiness and joy
to your faithful servants
come bride sabbath queen

Again and again, from the extraordinary allegorical creations of Juan de la Cruz, to the deeply esoteric, symbolically complex constructions of Yitzhak Luria, the erotic imagery of the Song of Songs proves its evocative power in endless elaboration. Whether by accident, or divine intent, this ancient poem celebrating the pain and exultation of erotic love—which somehow, against the odds, found its way into the biblical canon—has continued to inspire mystics of divine love across traditions, and seems likely to continue to do so for generations to come. They have claimed it and made it their own, and whisper to it now in their own private dialogue, just loud enough for us to overhear . . .

i crown you bride so holy
with secrets celestial
from the mating feast
of the angelic hosts

— Netanel Miles-Yépez
Crestone, Colorado
August 15th, 2017

biographies of the mystical poets

Shlomo Halevi Alkabetz (ca. 1500-1576) was a rabbi, kabbalist, and poet, best known for his liturgical poem, *Lekhah Dodi*. He was born in Salonica and later relocated to the community of kabbalists in Safed (S'fat).

Elazar Azikri (1533-1600) was a rabbi, kabbalist, and poet, best known for his liturgical poem, *Yedid Nefesh*, and for his ethical work, *Sefer Haredim*. He was born and lived his life in Safed (S'fat), active in the community of kabbalists there.

Yehudah Halevi (ca. 1075-1141) was a physician, philosopher, and arguabley the most important Jewish poet of Spain. As a philosopher, he is known for his work, *Sefer ha-Kuzari*. He was born in Toledo and died shortly after arriving in the Holy Land.

Yitzhak Luria (1534-1572), known as the *Ari ha-Kodesh*, the 'holy lion,' was a rabbi, and condsidered the preeminent kabbalist of his time, influencing all subsequent Kabbalah. He was born in Jerusalem and later died in Safed (S'fat), where he was the leader of the community of kabbalists.

Juan de Yepes y Alvarez (1542-1591), better known as Juan de la Cruz, was a Christian saint of the Carmelite Order (of Spanish-Jewish ancestry), known for his brilliant mystical writings, and considered the greatest poet of Spain. He was born in Fontiveros and died in Ubeda.

about the translator

Photo by Hilary Benas 2015

Netanel Miles-Yépez is an artist, philosopher, religion scholar, and Sufi spiritual teacher. Pir of the Inayati-Maimuni Order of Sufis, he is also co-director of Charis InterSpirituality, and lectures on both Sufism and InterSpritiuality around the United States. Netanel is likewise a professor in the Department of Religious Studies at Naropa University in Boulder, Colorado, and the executive editor of *Delumin/a—Spirituality. Culture. Arts.*